The Modern Witch's Journal

The Modern Witch's Journal

CHART YOUR MAGICKAL JOURNEY INTO HIDDEN WISDOM

Wendy Hobson

SIRIUS

SIRIUS

This edition published in 2019 by Sirius Publishing, a division of
Arcturus Publishing Limited,
26/27 Bickels Yard, 151–153 Bermondsey Street,
London SE1 3HA

ISBN: 978-1-78950-554-2
AD006695US

Printed in China

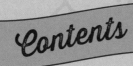

Contents

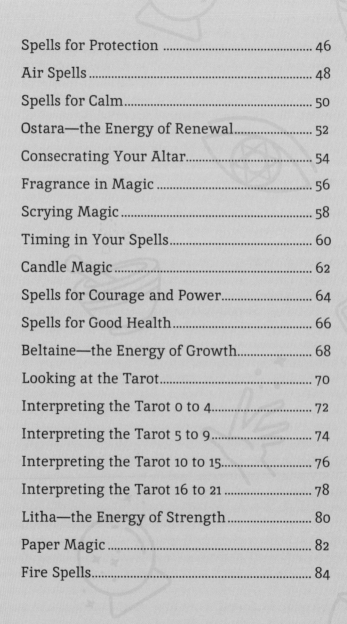

SETTING OUT
Your Road to Discovery

As the wheel of the
year turns, we all aim to fill our
lives fruitfully—working hard, enjoying
ourselves, staying healthy, learning, and
growing. Sometimes it works well, sometimes not.
But with every year that passes, we grow in experience,
and if we use that experience wisely, then we have the best
chance of making the next year even better.

This journal is designed to be your personal diary and notebook
to record the details of your journey. It will be unique to
you—your own Book of Shadows—and you can write down
anything you feel is important and adapt it in any way you
wish. You may like to stick mementos into the book—a
leaf that fell into your hand, a ticket to an event—or
add photographs or drawings. It is yours to
follow through, to dip into, and to start
and finish wherever you like.

What is Witchcraft?

Witchcraft has a long and illustrious history and has been practiced since ancient times. In Egypt, Africa, and Mesopotamia, among Native Americans and throughout Europe, people have contributed to our knowledge and understanding of witchcraft for thousands of years. Modern witchcraft aims to help you combine your psychic energies with those of the natural world, and then use that power to bring positive benefits to your life and strengthen your personality.

A Conversation with the Universe

Since magic is simply a way of communing with the energies of the universe, it makes sense that the lines of communication are as direct and uncomplicated as possible. Just like the children's joke in which the message "Send reinforcements, we are going to advance" comes out at the other end as "Send three and fourpence, we are going to a dance," the more people intervening in the communication, the more likely it is that it will be diluted or redirected. That means that it can be far more effective if you learn gradually and build up your own unique link to the universal energies rather than following spells by rote.

Where Do I Start?

A respect for the natural world and a belief in beauty and goodness are the cornerstones of witchcraft. When you start to practice your magical workings, begin by learning to use and trust your intuition. How do you respond to people, places, and activities? How much are you ruled by your heart or your head? Open your mind to possibilities and think about the essence of witchcraft and the positive benefits it can bring. You may wish to start at the beginning of this book, or you can move around the pages in whatever order you like. There is no right or wrong here—it is your journey. Enjoy.

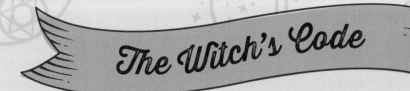

The Witch's Code

Every lifestyle system has its own set of rules: a driver's manual, if you like, to guide you on your path. The witch's code is known as the wiccan rede, and its function is to ensure that everyone maintains respect for themselves and each other. The rede contains much good advice and is usually written in verse. There are three essential points:

- Treat others as you expect to be treated yourself.
- Do what makes you happy as long as it doesn't harm anyone else.
- The energies you give out will come back threefold.

Have you obeyed the code?

Think about the last month. Write down some examples of how you have fulfilled the three main rules.

_____

_____

_____

_____

_____

_____

_____

What improvements would you like to make to your life?

_____

_____

_____

_____

_____

_____

_____

_____

_____

>>—> **How will you begin to make changes and still follow the code?**

_____

_____

_____

_____

_____

_____

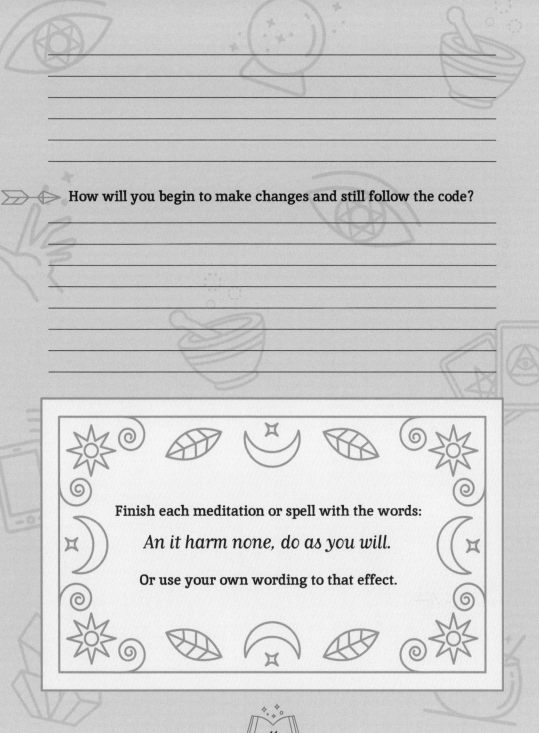

Finish each meditation or spell with the words:

An it harm none, do as you will.

Or use your own wording to that effect.

What Makes You a Witch?

Think about the personal qualities that make a successful witch. Be honest with yourself. Write down your strengths and weaknesses, and examples of how you demonstrate these good qualities. Then write down what you will do next month to improve on your weaknesses.

A witch is:

Loyal

Considerate

A good listener

A lover of nature

In tune with their inner self

Open-minded

Surrounded by like-minded people

A witch is not:

Greedy

Proud

Hypocritical

Bigoted

Selfish

Thoughtless

Unkind

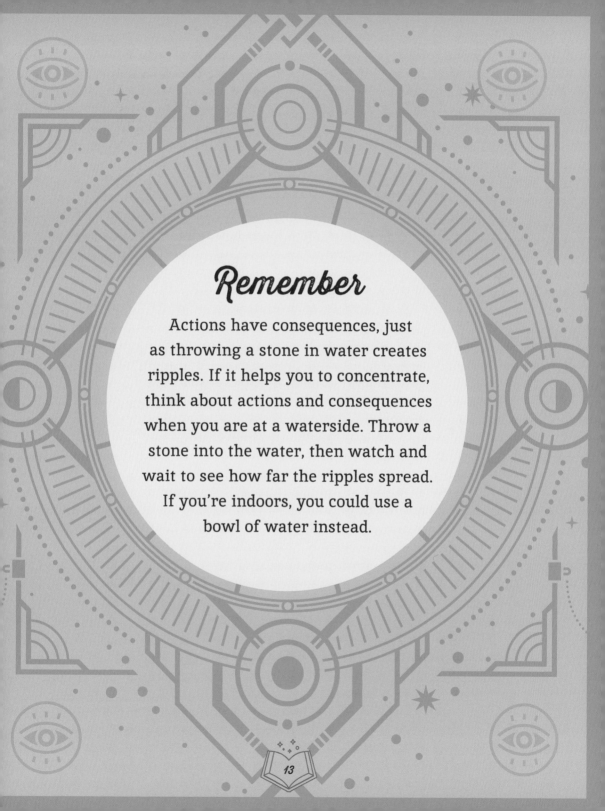

Remember

Actions have consequences, just
as throwing a stone in water creates
ripples. If it helps you to concentrate,
think about actions and consequences
when you are at a waterside. Throw a
stone into the water, then watch and
wait to see how far the ripples spread.
If you're indoors, you could use a
bowl of water instead.

Relax and Meditate

Bringing meditation skills into your life can have a hugely calming effect. Some people find it easy to focus; others find it harder. It is best to keep things simple. Be comfortable, focus on one image, and keep bringing your mind back to it if it wanders. A few minutes is long enough to begin with.

- Choose an image of yourself that looks positive and confident. This will be the focus for your meditation.
- Sit in a comfortable chair in a quiet, warm room, or lie on a bed.
- Tense your whole body, scrunch up your face, and make fists with your hands. Hold tightly for five seconds.
- Release the tension and let it soak away into the chair or bed.
- Keep the image in your mind as you picture yourself gently spreading across the chair or bed, completely relaxed.
- After five minutes, stretch your arms above your head to wake up your muscles.
- Drink a glass of water and sit quietly for a moment.
- Make some notes here on what helps you to meditate successfully.

✧ Location

_____

_____

_____

✧ Fragrances

_____

_____

_____

✧ *Light levels*

_____
_____
_____

✧ *Music*

_____
_____
_____

✧ *Background noise*

_____
_____
_____

✧ *Colors*

_____
_____
_____

✧ *Clothing*

_____
_____
_____

✧ *Images to focus on*

_____
_____
_____

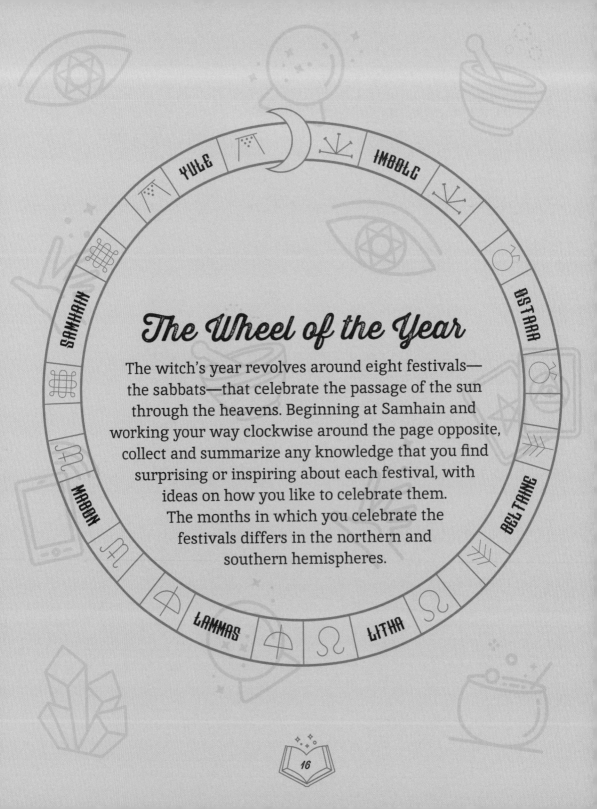

The Wheel of the Year

The witch's year revolves around eight festivals—the sabbats—that celebrate the passage of the sun through the heavens. Beginning at Samhain and working your way clockwise around the page opposite, collect and summarize any knowledge that you find surprising or inspiring about each festival, with ideas on how you like to celebrate them. The months in which you celebrate the festivals differs in the northern and southern hemispheres.

YULE

IMBOLC

OSTARA

BELTANE

LITHA

LAMMAS

MABON

SAMHAIN

SAMHAIN
Between autumn equinox and
winter solstice

Energy:_____

Color: _____

Element: _____

Theme:_____

Celebration: _____

Feelings: _____

YULE
Winter solstice

Energy:_____

Color: _____

Element: _____

Theme:_____

Celebration: _____

Feelings: _____

IMBOLC
Between winter solstice and
spring equinox

Energy:_____

Color: _____

Element: _____

Theme:_____

Celebration: _____

Feelings: _____

MABON
Autumn equinox

Energy:_____

Color: _____

Element: _____

Theme:_____

Celebration: _____

Feelings: _____

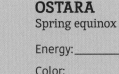

OSTARA
Spring equinox

Energy:_____

Color: _____

Element: _____

Theme:_____

Celebration: _____

Feelings: _____

LAMMAS
Between summer solstice and
autumn equinox

Energy:_____

Color: _____

Element: _____

Theme:_____

Celebration: _____

Feelings: _____

LITHA
Summer solstice

Energy:_____

Color: _____

Element: _____

Theme:_____

Celebration: _____

Feelings: _____

BELTAINE
Between spring equinox and
summer solstice

Energy:_____

Color: _____

Element: _____

Theme:_____

Celebration: _____

Feelings: _____

A Witch's Toolbox

What tools and equipment does a witch need? Very few, in fact, and you can use everyday items found around the home, preferably made of natural substances. Cleanse them in warm, soapy water before use, and leave them to dry in the sunshine. Keep them specifically for your spellcasting. Power-charge them overnight in the moonlight.

Here is a list of the basics of a witch's toolbox.

Amulets: Any objects that are protective or you feel are lucky, from ancient Egyptian ankhs to stones or crystals.

Baskets: To keep your items tidy and safe.

Bell: To ring at the beginning and end of a spell.

Book of Shadows: A record of all your spellcasting. Keep a special pen and use it just for writing down your spells.

Bowls: Use a gold bowl for the god, silver for the goddess, and place them on your altar.

Broom: To sweep away negative energy. Traditionally, a *besom* is made from a bundle of twigs tied around a stick.

Candles: A selection in different colors.

Cauldron: For mixing and for spells involving change.

Chalice: Any stemmed drinking glass to hold liquids during a spell, and to represent water.

Cords: For creating magic circles.

Crystals: To strengthen spells.

Essential oils and incense: For fragrance.

Knives: These are not essential; you can equally use a wand, your fingers, or even a chopstick. A knife represents fire, but you can use a candle or a blunt paper knife instead. Traditionally, an *athame* is a blunt double-edged knife with a black handle used to cut energy or open doors; a *boline* is a white-handled knife with a curved blade used for cutting herbs and so on; and a *burin* is a sharp stylus for inscribing candles.

Pentacle: A five-pointed star (pentagram) within a circle, a symbol that represents the earth. It is kept upright on your altar and is used to charge an object with energy. The four lower points on the star represent earth, air, fire, and water, with the top point representing the spirit.

Talisman: A magic-imbued symbol.

Wand: To draw magical symbols on the ground or in the air (the element to which it belongs), and to evoke magic.

Riding the Rainbow

Colors have a special significance in witchcraft. Each one elicits an intuitive response that relates to other aspects of magic, such as the four elements, the compass, chakras, sabbats, and so on.

Take some time out to meditate on the rainbow of colors, focusing on one color at a time. You'll find a simple technique on page 14. Feel the energies of the colors and note down how they make you feel and whether you agree with the type of magic they are generally considered suitable for, or whether they strike a different chord with you.

Remember that you can use colors in your surroundings, in images, candles, crystals, your clothes, or your altar decorations.

Pink
Friendship, romance, virtue, and contentment

Red
Courage, strength, and determination

Orange
Confidence, enthusiasm, and energy

Yellow
Communication and knowledge

Green
Nurturing, growth, security, and good luck

Light blue
Tranquillity, good
health, and calm

_____
_____
_____
_____

Blue
Intuition, emotion,
and wisdom

_____
_____
_____
_____

Purple
Psychic development
and personal strength

_____
_____
_____
_____

Grey
Compromise and
self-protection

_____
_____
_____
_____

White
Innocence, honesty,
and protection

_____
_____
_____
_____

Black
Closing and
transitions

_____
_____
_____
_____

Brown
Stability, strength, and
sound decisions

_____
_____
_____
_____

Gold
Good fortune and
masculine power

_____
_____
_____
_____

Silver
Insight and femininity

_____
_____
_____
_____

21

Spells for Inner Beauty

The old adage says "beauty is in the eye of the beholder." This is very true. Whether we are looking at a painting, at a person, or looking at ourselves in the mirror, we all see something slightly different. But if we see beauty at the core of everyone, then the details cease to matter.

We all have something about ourselves—or perhaps many things—that we don't like, but fundamentally what we need to like is ourselves, the whole package. You can do many things to make yourself look your best: wear the right colors and shapes to suit you, have your hair done, or perhaps use some makeup. All of these things make a difference to how we perceive ourselves and how others perceive us. But the most important thing is what's inside, and it's far more effective to work on bolstering your self-esteem than to wish for a different-shaped nose or a better figure.

The general theme of love and beauty uses red and pink colors, sun images, and anything that grows and bolsters confidence. Spells might include gaining confidence in your own ability, being positive about your prospects, helping you to look for love, or putting you in the right frame of mind for a special occasion.

Look at A Spell Template (page 44) and the Table of Correspondences (page 124) and write your own confidence and inner beauty spells on the page opposite.

Inner beauty spell

Inner beauty spell

Inner beauty spell

Inner beauty spell

Following the Sun

We are all familiar with the zodiac signs (or sun signs) in astrology, and witches believe in the qualities of energy that relate to each one. The signs also interact with the energies of the four elements.

Observe people you know and practice assessing their zodiac sign. Note the common characteristics and the differences, and use these to help you relate to the people more effectively.

△ Fire signs

Aries: Adventurous, independent

_____

_____

Leo: Enthusiastic, expressive

_____

_____

Sagittarius: Energetic, optimistic

_____

_____

▽ Earth signs

Taurus: Practical, sensual

_____

_____

Virgo: Analytical, precise

_____

_____

Capricorn: Determined, traditional

_____

_____

△ *Air signs*

Gemini: Quick-witted, mercurial

_____

_____

Libra: Kind, peaceful

_____

_____

Aquarius: Independent, friendly

_____

_____

▽ *Water signs*

Cancer: Empathetic, feeling

_____

_____

Scorpio: Focused, ambitious

_____

_____

Pisces: Generous, genuine

_____

_____

Casting a Circle

Before you begin a spell, cast a circle around yourself to contain the magic and protect you from distractions and outside influences. You can use something physical, such as a rope, or simply walk around a circumference or indicate it with a wand or your hand.

- The location will determine what is most suitable.
- Make sure the circle is large enough to contain anything that you have decided to use or do in your spell.
- Any boundary markers—such as rope, potted plants, stones, twigs, crystals, or wooden items—should relate to the particular spell you are working.
- Make sure there are no safety considerations if you are using potentially dangerous items such as candles.
- Indicate the circle or walk around it, saying words such as:

   This is my circle, my circle of power
   To contain the magic I release this hour.

- Jot down some notes to use when you are spellcasting.

❖ What the circle has to contain

_____
_____
_____
_____
_____

❖ Good places to cast a magic circle

_____
_____
_____
_____
_____

❖ Suitable items to mark the edge of a circle

_____
_____
_____
_____
_____

❖ Suitable verses to open a circle

_____
_____
_____
_____
_____

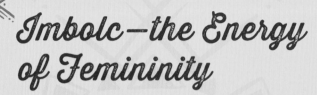

Imbolc—the Energy of Femininity

Imbolc is the festival celebrated halfway between the winter solstice and the spring equinox, when the natural world is just beginning to unleash its potential for growth. Winter is over and spring is beginning, so this festival is associated with the east, where the sun rises.

Good spells to perform around this time would be those promoting any kind of growth or development in your life, your outlook, your relationships, or your career. Make notes on the spells you cast at this time. Look at A Spell Template (page 44) and the Table of Correspondences (page 124) for more ideas.

Imbolc spell

_____

_____

_____

_____

_____

_____

_____

_____

Imbolc spell

_____

_____

_____

_____

_____

_____

_____

_____

◈▶ *Imbolc spell*

_____

_____

_____

_____

_____

_____

_____

_____

_____

◈▶ *Imbolc spell*

_____

_____

_____

_____

_____

_____

_____

_____

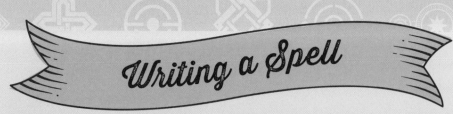

Writing a Spell

Some spells can be performed in a very casual and intuitive way; off the cuff, if you like. Others need very careful planning and consideration. For these, there are certain issues you need to think about. Write down what you think is most important by answering the following questions.

Target: Who is the spell for?

_____

_____

_____

_____

Objective: What is the spell aiming to achieve?

_____

_____

_____

_____

Rules: Does the spell obey the rules?

_____

_____

_____

_____

Focus: What is your focus object to encourage concentration?

_____

_____

_____
_____
_____
_____

○ **Anticipated outcome:** What would you like to happen?

_____
_____
_____
_____
_____

○ **Potential issues:** What could go wrong?

_____
_____
_____
_____
_____

○ **Grounding:** How will you complete the spell?

_____
_____
_____
_____
_____

○ **Action:** What can you do to encourage the energies?

_____
_____
_____
_____
_____

Love Spells

When you are writing a love spell, it is more personal and heartfelt than any other. The energies should be soft and opening, strongly resonating to the color pink. You may like to perform these spells indoors or outside, depending on the situation, but the location should be a beautiful and calm place. To be loved, it is said that we must first learn to love ourselves, so make that a priority.

Look at A Spell Template (page 44) and the Table of Correspondences (page 124) to guide you in creating your own love spells. This type of magic often involves inscribing candles or using ribbons to link two people together. Strands of hair and fragrant essential oils also feature.

In writing a love spell, you may be looking for romance, to win someone's affection, to forge a new relationship or strengthen an existing one, to ignite passion or find companionship.

Love spell

_____

_____

_____

_____

_____

_____

_____

_____

_____

_____

_____

Love spell

_____
_____
_____
_____
_____
_____
_____
_____

Love spell

_____
_____
_____
_____
_____
_____
_____
_____
_____

Love spell

_____
_____
_____
_____
_____
_____
_____
_____

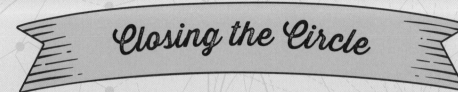

Closing the Circle

Once you have finished a spell, you should close the magic circle that you opened at the start. This is to ground yourself and complete the spell, returning all the elemental energies to their rightful places.

The best way of achieving this closure is to reverse the ritual that you used when setting up the spell: blow out any candles, speak a release to the four elements, then walk counterclockwise around the circle. You could also ring a bell to dissipate the energy and, if you wish, recite some closing verses. Try the sample verse on the page opposite, or make up your own closing rituals and verses and write them here.

☾ Closing rituals

_____

_____

_____

_____

_____

_____

_____

_____

_____

_____

_____

_____

_____

☾ Closing verses

The magic is done, no spirits offended,

Return to your place, now the problem's been tended.

Take down the circle, release the power,

With thanks to the elements for their help this hour.

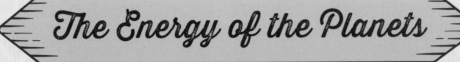

The Energy of the Planets

We have already seen that the sun plays a key role in spellcasting, but the planets can also have an influence if you tune into their energies. Make notes here on how you use planetary energies in your spellcasting, along with photographic images or visualizations.

☿ **Mercury:** Communication

_____

_____

_____

_____

♀ **Venus:** Love and relationships

_____

_____

_____

_____

_____

⊕ **Earth:** Practicality

_____

_____

_____

_____

_____

♂ Mars: Assertiveness and power

_____
_____
_____
_____

♃ Jupiter: Prosperity and control

_____
_____
_____
_____

♄ Saturn: Releasing negativity

_____
_____
_____
_____

♅ Uranus: The power of change

_____
_____
_____
_____

♆ Neptune: Balance and moving forward

_____
_____
_____
_____

Talking to the Elements

How should you address the four elements in your spellcasting? Earth, air, fire, and water provide a channel to natural powers, so you need to address them with respect and in a way that helps you to focus your mind on their best qualities. When making a spell, you need to take

Earth

Positive	Negative
Stability	*Pig-headedness*

Air

Positive	Negative
Intelligent	*Irresponsible*

into account the particular aspects of each element's power which you wish to utilize. Remember that all the elements have negative as well as positive aspects. If you are looking for stability, for example, don't go overboard into pig-headedness or stubbornness.

Write down some positive words to use in your spells and some negative words to avoid, following the examples shown here.

Fire

Positive	Negative
Powerful	*Angry*
_____	_____
_____	_____
_____	_____
_____	_____
_____	_____
_____	_____
_____	_____

Water

Positive	Negative
Flexible	*Unstable*
_____	_____
_____	_____
_____	_____
_____	_____
_____	_____
_____	_____

Powerful Days

Choose the right day of the week to perform your spells, to maximize their power and enhance the flow of energy. Make a note of the spells that you have performed successfully on particular days.

Monday The day of the moon dedicated to home, family, and everything feminine.

_____

_____

_____

_____

Tuesday Dedicated to Mars, so ideal for spells of confidence, power, and energy.

_____

_____

_____

_____

Wednesday All about communication, study, and speed on the day dedicated to Mercury, the winged messenger.

_____

_____

_____

_____

Thursday Money and prosperity are favored on a Thursday, overseen by Jupiter, the ruler of the gods.

_____
_____
_____
_____

Friday The day of Venus, so the best day to choose for all kinds of love and relationship spells.

_____
_____
_____
_____

Saturday Saturn's day is ideal for breaking bad habits, repelling negative influences, and instilling self-discipline.

_____
_____
_____
_____

Sunday The sun's day can be dedicated to any magic, but particularly that involving you and your happiness.

_____
_____
_____
_____

Spells for Relationships

Look at A Spell Template (page 44) and the Table of Correspondences (page 124) and create your own spells to cement relationships with friends or family, or to resolve differences after an argument.

It is important that your spells are unique to you, so while you can take information and advice from all kinds of sources, making spells that are your own is far more satisfying and effective.

The feel of the spells should always be uplifting and encouraging, so include lots of positive energy, perhaps with a touch of banishing of the negative. Good places to work your spells are those that you associate with being friendly and sociable.

Relationship spells are often related to communication, so as well as using Venus and doing your spell on a Friday, think about whether it would be useful to bring in air and Mercury images, or use wind or images of birds when working your spells.

Relationship spell

_____

_____

_____

_____

_____

_____

_____

_____

Relationship spell

_____
_____
_____
_____
_____
_____

Relationship spell

_____
_____
_____
_____
_____
_____
_____
_____
_____

Relationship spell

_____
_____
_____
_____
_____
_____
_____
_____
_____

A Spell Template

This journal is all about creating your own individual and unique spells, each one containing a range of elements that combine to make the magic as strong and effective as it can be.

For each spell you create, choose a selection of the most appropriate items, known as correspondences, that will strengthen the magic. For example, a spell for a new job might include gold, fire, and an image of a dragon, and be performed at noon to maximize the positive energies.

Correspondences

Make notes on correspondences that you find particularly successful.

Colors
_____
_____
_____
_____

Fragrance
_____
_____
_____
_____

Sun sign
_____
_____
_____
_____

Crystals
_____
_____
_____
_____

Location
_____
_____
_____
_____

Time of day
_____
_____
_____
_____

Direction
_____
_____
_____
_____

Phase of the moon
_____
_____
_____
_____

Verses
_____
_____
_____
_____

Element
_____
_____
_____
_____

Sabbat
_____
_____
_____
_____

Zodiac sign
_____
_____
_____
_____

Energy
_____
_____
_____
_____

Season
_____
_____
_____
_____

Feel free to
copy this page for
personal use.

Spells for Protection

You may sometimes need to ask for help for general protection because you are feeling vulnerable or, more specifically, to protect you from unkindness or unwanted attention.

Visualization plays a strong role when you request the support and guidance of the goddess or an angel in protective spells. Use white candles and evoke the energies of the elements to bring their specific powers to help you. Protective circles can be drawn around you at waist level, moving the index finger of your dominant hand in a clockwise direction. You could imagine yourself in a huge bubble of protection so that any harmful energy simply bounces back to be absorbed by the giver.

Look at A Spell Template (page 44) and the Table of Correspondences (page 124) and create your own protective spells. Example spells might be to protect yourself from bullies, from the unwanted attention of someone, for protection from harm, or to protect yourself from negative influences on you or your loved ones.

Protection spell

_____

_____

_____

_____

_____

_____

_____

_____

Protection spell

_____
_____
_____
_____
_____
_____
_____
_____

Protection spell

_____
_____
_____
_____
_____
_____
_____
_____
_____
_____

Air Spells

Air spells are ideally carried out in the open air, but if that is not possible, bring fresh air into the room by opening a window. If it is a windy day when you're doing your spell, that's even better, because you can feel and hear the energy of the air all around you.

Take advantage of the wind, close your eyes, and focus 100 percent on the sounds you hear. Don't try to identify them individually. Let go of your conscious mind and listen to the sounds as you would listen to a piece of music—as a wonderful, coherent whole. You might want to use the occasion for an impromptu spell, or simply to feel at one with the energies flowing around you and through you.

You may wish to recite some verses:

Air clear, wind strong
As the leaves blow along
Blow away a care or three
And let them not come back to me.

Look at the spells relating to Paper Magic too (page 82), since they can be particularly effective on a windy day.

Air spell

_____
_____
_____
_____
_____
_____
_____

Air spell

_____
_____
_____
_____
_____
_____
_____

Air spell

_____
_____
_____
_____
_____
_____
_____

Spells for Calm

We all need to slow down and calm down from time to time, but for some of us anxiety can be a real problem and one that must first be addressed with practical steps. Using meditation and visualization can help, so try to work out a sequence that suits you and which you can call on at a moment's notice.

If you begin with the full relaxation process and repeat it regularly, you should gradually find that it becomes easier and more instinctive. At some point you will realize that you have actually been going through the process without thinking about it—much like when you're learning to drive a car and suddenly appreciate that you've been changing gear automatically without spelling out the process step by step in your head.

To begin, sit or lie in a comfortable place where you will not be disturbed. Gentle sunlight and warmth are both good. You may like to enhance the atmosphere with some scented candles or incense.

Look at A Spell Template (page 44) and the Table of Correspondences (page 124) and create your own calming spells. These might include helping you through a nerve-racking event such as an interview, supporting any stressful dealings with a particular person, or improving your reactions to demanding situations.

○ *Calming spell*

_____
_____
_____
_____

○ *Calming spell*

_____
_____
_____
_____

○ *Calming spell*

_____
_____
_____
_____

○ *Calming spell*

_____
_____
_____
_____

Ostara—the Energy of Renewal

Ostara is the festival of the spring equinox, based on the Celtic spring festivals for Eostre and the Christian Easter. The keynotes are the explosion of new growth, fertility, and exuberant energy, so this is the ideal occasion for casting spells relating to renewal, birth, reawakening, and self-transformation. Making an Ostara altar is a fun thing to do at this time.

✷ Ostara spell

_____
_____
_____
_____
_____
_____
_____

✷ Ostara spell

_____
_____
_____
_____

Ostara spell

Ostara spell

Consecrating Your Altar

If you already have a special spell-making space, this can become an altar with a little more attention. Think about your altar carefully and set it up with consideration and precision. Once you have consecrated it, no one else should touch it or its contents, otherwise all items will need to be cleansed and consecrated again. This ritual drives off negative energies and ensures that you begin your magic on a clean sheet.

- Cleanse and empower your magical items.
- Lay an altar cloth on your altar, then stand a pentacle at the back, with a silver and a gold candle in front to represent the god and the goddess.
- Position an earth image in the north, air in the east, fire in the south, and water in the west.
- Cleanse your altar three times with a broom—once for the physical, once for the emotional, and a final time for the psychic.
- Sprinkle the boundary circle with water, working clockwise.
- Light a stick of incense that is appropriate to the location and your own personality.
- Light the silver candle while saying the following words, or make up your own:

> *Lady of the silver moon, bless this site and make it mine.*

- Light the golden candle and say these words, or make up your own:

  > *Lord of the sun, with shining power, give me strength to do good*
  > *every hour.*
  > *An it harm none, so let it be.*

- Address each element individually by moving your hand, pentacle, or wand clockwise over the element, saying words such as:

  > *Earth, give me strength and stability,*
  > *Air, brush my heart with your knowledge,*
  > *Fire, bring me passion and power,*
  > *Water, cleanse my heart with your shower.*

- When all the negative energies have dispersed, say:

  > *Move off, move off, move away negativity.*
  > *An it harm none, do as you wish.*

- Bless the altar.
- Sit in front of the lighted candles, staring into the flames to imprint the image on your mind's eye.
- Close your eyes but maintain the image of the flames. Visualize the power of the god and the goddess moving into the space until it fills the area completely.
- Ring a bell four times to send the power to the altar and make it ready for your spells.

Fragrance in Magic

It is often said that our sense of smell is the most powerfully evocative of all the senses, having the ability to set a mood or recall an atmosphere like no other. It is therefore an important tool in the witch's armory and a major factor in creating the backdrop for your spells.

Different fragrances have different effects, so test out various options and see which ones work best for you. Start by trying some common fragrances (listed below with the atmospheres they tend to induce) and make notes on how you react to them, then begin to expand your repertoire by including more unusual scents. To create scents, you can use fragrant candles, incense cones, oil burners, or essential oils.

Chamomile: Relaxing

_____
_____
_____

Lavender: Calming and relaxing

_____
_____
_____
_____

Orange: Refreshing and good for dispelling negativity

_____
_____
_____

Peppermint: Uplifting and stress-reducing

_____
_____
_____
_____

Rose: Romantic and healing

_____
_____
_____
_____

Rosemary: Energy-boosting

_____
_____
_____
_____

Sage: For sharpening concentration and attention

_____
_____
_____
_____

Sandalwood: Soothing and good for meditation

_____
_____
_____
_____

Other fragrances

_____
_____

Scrying Magic

This very old form of magic is a water-based tool, so it is especially good when seeking guidance on emotional issues. Make a cup of tea with loose leaves, then ask a specific question while you drink the tea. Swirl the cup around seven times clockwise, then let the leaves settle. Working clockwise from the handle, the relevance of the tea leaf patterns starts in the past and spirals down into the future.

Pattern interpretation is complex, but the following general guidelines will get you started in making your own tea leaf readings. In time, you can add notes on your own interpretations.

Animals

Generally favorable, indicating hard work and success, although generally unpopular animals, such as rats, are not good, and reptiles indicate arguments.

Birds

Good luck, especially swans, but not owls.

Circular shapes

Good, particularly in finances.

Crossed or angular shapes

Troublesome.

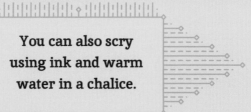

You can also scry using ink and warm water in a chalice.

Flowers or trees

Good luck, contentment, and growth.

Letters

News.

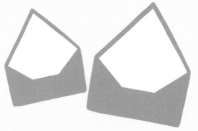

Linear patterns

Travel or movement.

People

Generally positive.

Sharp items

Knives, saws, or any sharp instruments suggest arguments.

Vehicles

Suggest travel or visits.

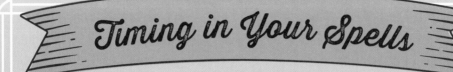

Timing in Your Spells

Choose the season most appropriate to your spell—spring for growth, summer for warmth, autumn for abundance, and winter for stability and development. The moon phase is also important, so that you use the waxing moon for development and the waning moon for calm.

The time of day makes a difference too. To help you choose the best times for your spellmaking, jot down notes about particularly successful spells you have made at specific times of the day.

Dawn

This is the time for spells involving growth, development, and new beginnings, such as finding a new job, a new home or a new partner.

_____

_____

_____

_____

_____

_____

Noon

The day's energies are at their height, so noon is the best time for spells requiring power, such as asking for strength to face a difficult situation.

_____

_____

_____

_____

_____

_____

_____

Dusk

This is the time for spells of releasing, reducing, and letting go—for example ending a difficult relationship or saying farewell to someone who is dear to you.

_____

_____

_____

_____

_____

_____

Midnight

This is a powerful time for spells relating to overcoming or banishing obstacles. You might cast a spell at midnight for getting over a major hurdle or difficulty in your life.

_____

_____

_____

_____

_____

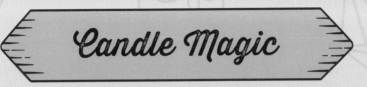

Candle Magic

You will almost certainly include candles in many of your spells, always remembering to be safe when using them. They provide color and often fragrance, they bring beauty to your spells and help you to focus and concentrate, and they are the perfect representation of the element of fire. These attributes can be helpful in any spellmaking, as spells all need power or enthusiasm of some kind to succeed.

The candle actually combines references to each of the four elements: earth in the wax, air in the breath to extinguish it, fire in the flame, and water in the liquid wax. It is therefore a very potent symbol that you can buy in almost any suitable color and in many fragrances. Note that fragrant candles lose their potency over time, so don't store them for too long. You can also inscribe candles with a word or a name to bring extra power to your spell. Simply use a sharp object such as a bodkin or thick needle.

Write about your most successful candle spells here.

Candle spell

_____

_____

_____

_____

_____

_____

_____

_____

_____

Candle spell

_____
_____
_____
_____
_____
_____
_____

Candle spell

_____
_____
_____
_____
_____
_____
_____
_____

Candle spell

_____
_____
_____
_____
_____
_____
_____

Spells for Courage and Power

These spells are all about confidence, and this is something you should aim to build up gradually. If you are a naturally strong and confident person, you can go straight into spells of power with dragons, fire, sunshine, and energy at their heart. However, if you are a more shy and retiring type of person, it is no use casting spells to help you get a CEO's job. Begin smaller and more modestly to gradually develop your confidence, then get bolder slowly and you will achieve more as a result.

Spells might include wanting to gain a promotion or finding the courage to face a difficult meeting or make a hard decision. Look at A Spell Template (page 44) and the Table of Correspondences (page 124) and create your own spells to enhance your courage and power.

Courage spell

_____

_____

_____

_____

_____

_____

_____

_____

_____

_____

_____

_____

✦ Courage spell

_____
_____
_____
_____
_____
_____
_____
_____

✦ Courage spell

_____
_____
_____
_____
_____
_____
_____
_____
_____

✦ Courage spell

_____
_____
_____
_____
_____
_____
_____
_____

Spells for Good Health

Healing spells might include wanting to maintain or improve your own health or that of someone else, to help with a specific medical problem, or to find the strength to support someone through serious illness.

Look at A Spell Template (page 44) and the Table of Correspondences (page 124) and create your own health spells. They should be uplifting and encouraging, so include lots of positive energy, perhaps with a touch of banishing of the negative. Good places are those you associate with good health—the park, the garden, and so on. Sometimes you may want to be in a medical environment, but try to maintain the positive energies. Healing spells frequently involve candle magic but also herbs and flowers, and they are particularly effective under the new moon.

☼ Health spell

_____
_____
_____
_____
_____
_____
_____

☼ Health spell

_____
_____
_____

※ *Health spell*

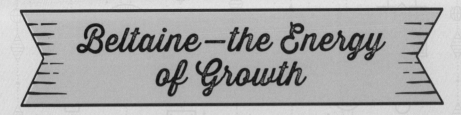

Beltaine—the Energy of Growth

Beltaine is the moon festival that occurs halfway between the spring equinox and the summer solstice, so in the northern hemisphere it usually coincides with May Day, which has modern political significance but has been celebrated as a spring festival in Europe for hundreds of years.

It is a time when the earth energies are at their strongest, bringing abundance and dispersing any negative winter energies, so it is a good time for doing earth magic: spells for stability, finding practical solutions, and developing projects.

 *Beltaine spell*

_____

_____

_____

_____

_____

_____

_____

_____

_____

✧ *Beltaine spell*

_____

_____

_____

_____

_____

_____

_____

_____

✧ *Beltaine spell*

_____

_____

_____

_____

_____

_____

_____

_____

Looking at the Tarot

At any time in your journey, you can stop to take stock of your situation and the direction you want your life to take. Are you contented? Is this how you wanted your life to go? Using tarot cards is one way of answering these questions. Tarot is an ancient and complex study, and here we merely scratch the surface to give you a potential entry point.

A full tarot pack contains 78 cards in all. The major arcana is made up of 22 named cards. The minor arcana contains cards numbered one to ten, plus four picture cards in each of four suits: swords, wands, discs, and cups. Start with the major arcana only.

Since it is impossible to be totally objective about oneself, you might ask someone else to read your cards for you. Look at the meanings on the pages that follow to complete your reading. Upright cards relate to how you experience events and how you express yourself and relate to those around you. Upside-down cards describe what you are feeling inside.

Frame your thoughts into a specific question. Shuffle the major arcana cards, cut them, then lay them out face down in the sequence illustrated, which is known as the Celtic cross. Each of the cards represents an aspect of your question.

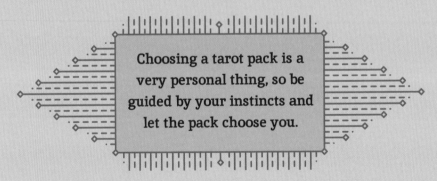

Choosing a tarot pack is a very personal thing, so be guided by your instincts and let the pack choose you.

5
what you are
aiming for

10
the likely
outcome unless
you make
changes

3
how the
situation came
about

1
what is
happening
now and how
you feel about
it

4
the most
likely next
step

9
your hopes
and fears

8
external
influences
beyond your
control

2
the main
challenge to
be resolved

6
underlying
feelings

7
where to seek
advice

71

Interpreting the Tarot 0 to 4

Look carefully at your tarot images. Meditate on each card. Try to see beyond the basic images and think about the detail and symbolism. What do you see in the images? How can you apply that to your life?

0 | Fool

Be confident and optimistic about the new projects ahead of you. Grasp opportunities and don't look back.

_____
_____
_____
_____
_____
_____

1 | Magus

You have the power to achieve your goals, as long as you make sure you think through the consequences of what you intend to do.

_____
_____
_____
_____
_____

2 Priestess

You may be unaware of something that will help you to solve your problem. Trust your intuition rather than what you think you know or what other people tell you.

_____

_____

_____

_____

_____

3 Empress

Stay in touch with your creative side in order to maximize your emotional growth.

_____

_____

_____

_____

_____

_____

4 Emperor

Perhaps you need to break free from the constraints of your circumstances, or simply strengthen and secure your foundations.

_____

_____

_____

_____

_____

Interpreting the Tarot 5 to 9

Do not lose sight of the fact that tarot cards contain symbolic images representing the energies of the universe, and you need to interpret them to apply the images to your specific question. The hermit does not mean that you will be alone any more than the lovers mean that you will meet a tall, dark, handsome stranger. What do you see in the images?

5 Hierophant

If you feel the need for a spiritual teacher, one may come to you. However, remember to trust your own knowledge and the fact that you can increase your knowledge by study.

_____

_____

_____

_____

_____

6 Lovers

Learn to love yourself first, as this will impact on all your partnerships of any kind. It will also help you balance the aspects of your personality.

_____

_____

_____

_____

7 Chariot

If you plan well, your vibrant personality will help you overcome any obstacles you find in front of you.

_____

_____

_____

_____

_____

_____

8 Adjustment

Changes may be on the horizon. These will be most beneficial if you are calm, so look to find your inner stillness.

_____

_____

_____

_____

_____

9 Hermit

Use this opportunity to resolve past problems so that you can move forward. This may involve withdrawing or studying.

_____

_____

_____

_____

_____

Interpreting the Tarot
10 to 15

This group contains the most universally misunderstood card of all, generally eliciting an ominous "dah, dah, DAH" sound effect in mystery plays. But death is not an end; it is a closing stage that will then allow a new phase to emerge. What do you see in the images?

10 Lust

Use your passion to overcome obstacles in your path, but do not let it get out of control.

_____
_____
_____
_____
_____

11 Fortune

Be alert for sudden changes—positive or negative.

_____
_____
_____
_____

12 Hanged man

Let go of past fears or difficult issues so that you can progress.

_____
_____

_____

_____

_____

13 Death

This does not literally mean death of any kind, but more the liberating end of a phase of your life, which can be transformative.

_____

_____

_____

_____

_____

14 Art

Seek to understand how the elements of your life can be balanced.

_____

_____

_____

_____

_____

15 Devil

Break away from materialism or situations that you know are not doing you any good.

_____

_____

_____

_____

_____

Interpreting the Tarot 16 to 21

Remember that all of the interpretations in these pages are merely suggested as guidelines to start you off on your study of tarot; they are not meant as ends in themselves. What do you see in the images?

16 Tower

Be aware of your current reality and don't cling on to the past. This may be briefly painful, but you need to be yourself.

_____

_____

_____

_____

_____

17 Star

Through gentle healing, you should find resolution and inner peace.

_____

_____

_____

_____

_____

18 Moon

Take responsibility for yourself and your actions, and don't be afraid to examine your behavior from all angles.

_____

_____

_____

_____

_____

_____

_____

19 *Sun*

Seize opportunities, as the present moment is potentially a great time for relationships, harmony, and feeling warm and happy.

_____

_____

_____

_____

20 *Aeon*

A change is on the horizon, but you already know that. Use your true understanding to make decisions and avoid being judgmental.

_____

_____

_____

_____

21 *Universe*

Remember that you don't always need to achieve—you can just "be."

_____

_____

_____

_____

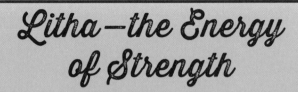

Litha—the Energy of Strength

The name of the festival of light at the summer solstice means "sun standing still." The longest day of the year obviously highlights the height of the power of the sun, celebrating everything that is strong and elemental. It is traditionally associated with the god and with everything masculine.

Keynotes for Litha spells are related to strength, determination, and courage. You may choose to cast spells requesting the strength to face difficult situations, to restore your power to an unequal relationship, or to move forward with your job prospects.

Look at A Spell Template (page 44) and the Table of Correspondences (page 124) and create spells to help you in the way you need most.

✦ Litha spell

_____

_____

_____

_____

_____

_____

_____

_____

_____

_____

_____

_____

✵ Litha spell

_____
_____
_____
_____
_____
_____
_____
_____

✵ Litha spell

_____
_____
_____
_____
_____
_____
_____
_____
_____
_____

✵ Litha spell

_____
_____
_____
_____
_____
_____
_____

Paper Magic

Words can be very powerful in magic, so you must always think very carefully when you are writing a spell, particularly if the words form a mantra that you will be repeating.

You can create a paper magic tree in two or three dimensions, then tie or stick on leaves on which you have written wishes or hopes that you would like to fulfill. For every wish, make two other leaves and write on each one a way in which you will try to make that wish come true, thus adding leaves to the tree in threes.

Another good way to release yourself from situations or people holding you back is to write a few words describing what you don't want in your life on leaves (or strips of rice paper that will quickly biodegrade), then punch holes in the leaves with a hole punch and thread them very loosely on the tail of a kite. Launch the kite on a windy day, and as the leaves blow away from your kite, say words such as:

> *Air clear, wind strong, blow away a care or three*
> *And let them not come back to me*
> *And let them not come back to me*
> *For I want to be clear and free.*

➤➤⟶ *Paper spell*

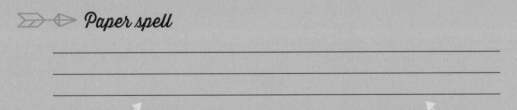

82

Paper spell

___

Paper spell

___

Paper spell

___

Fire Spells

Aligned with the sun and all the assertive energies, fire is the element that most represents raw strength and power. As such, it has great potential, but it must also be handled with care lest it become more aggressive than assertive.

Look at A Spell Template (page 44) and the Table of Correspondences (page 124) and create your own fire spells. They might relate to wanting a promotion at work, looking for courage to make a difficult decision, or asking for the strength to help you when caring for family or friends.

Fire spell

_____
_____
_____
_____
_____
_____
_____
_____

Fire spell

_____
_____
_____
_____

△ Fire spell

_____

△ Fire spell

_____

Although it sounds rather pedestrian, safety has to be your primary consideration here. Whether you are using a fire or candles outside or indoors, you must be sure you are using them safely, and that any flames or hot materials are completely extinguished when you have finished.

A Personal Charm or Amulet

Many people carry a charm with them to bring them good luck, such as the symbol of a four-leaf clover or a horseshoe, but you can use anything that makes you feel positive.

Jot down all the kinds of lucky charms you can think of. If you don't already carry a charm—perhaps on your keyring—then you might like to bless one to carry with you and help to bring some good fortune your way.

At the end of the exercise, make notes about your chosen charm and the reasons why you have selected it. Describe it in detail and make a drawing of it. It doesn't matter if you think you're not very good at art; the object is to help you to really look at the object in minute detail.

✦ Animal charms

_____

_____

_____

_____

_____

✦ Popular charms

_____

_____

_____

_____
_____
_____
_____

✦ Personal charms

_____
_____
_____
_____
_____

✦ Character charms

_____
_____
_____
_____
_____
_____
_____

✦ My chosen charm

_____
_____
_____
_____
_____
_____

Spells for the Workplace

Workplace spells could include all kinds of components, depending on the nature of the spell. If you are looking for promotion, for example, you might focus on the energies of the new, so you could look for yellows, white, and silver; perform the spell at dawn during the new moon; and invoke the element air. If you're resolving arguments, then you might look toward the blue spectrum, where you will find balance and compromise.

Look at A Spell Template (page 44) and the Table of Correspondences (page 124) and create your own workplace spells. Examples might be to improve the atmosphere after a difficult argument, to ask for a pay increase, to resolve differences with a colleague or boss, to find a new job, or to prepare for an interview.

◄○► *Workplace spell*

_____
_____
_____
_____
_____
_____
_____

◄○► *Workplace spell*

_____
_____
_____

_____

_____

_____

_____

◉ *Workplace spell*

_____

_____

_____

_____

_____

_____

_____

◉ *Workplace spell*

_____

_____

_____

_____

_____

_____

_____

_____

Lammas—the Energy of Abundance

The festival of Lammas falls midway between the summer solstice and the autumn equinox, marking the end of the summer and the beginning of the autumn. Being the first harvest festival, it is a time to celebrate the gathering of the harvest and the assessment of the vital energies of the earth. Lammas is a good time to take stock of what you have achieved in the previous few months, and to thank the earth for the good it has brought you.

Spells to cast at this time relate to promoting abundance, so you might be looking for a pay rise at work, developing a business, or moving into a larger home. Look at A Spell Template (page 44) and the Table of Correspondences (page 124) and create your own spells.

✦ Lammas spell

_____

_____

_____

_____

_____

_____

✦ Lammas spell

_____

_____

_____

_____

_____

_____

_____

_____

_____

✧ *Lammas spell*

_____

_____

_____

_____

_____

_____

_____

_____

_____

✧ *Lammas spell*

_____

_____

_____

_____

_____

_____

_____

_____

_____

_____

Chakra Energy

Originating in Eastern philosophy, the seven chakras are the seven centers of energy running down the middle of the body. Energy flows through them and around the body, and when it flows freely, you feel balanced and healthy. If the channels become blocked, you may feel prevented from moving forward, or even unwell.

The chakras both absorb and transmit energy, so you are affected by the energy of your surroundings or the people you are with, as well as affecting external events and people yourself. The seven chakras are:

- **Crown:** Knowledge and mental activity are stimulated by this chakra point on the top of the head.
- **Brow:** Right between the eyes is often called the third eye chakra, which is the heart of intuition and clear-sightedness.
- **Throat:** Trust is crucial here, as is the ability to communicate your thoughts and feelings, and understand those of others.
- **Heart:** Love, compassion, empathy, and self-esteem are housed nearest to the heart.
- **Solar plexus:** Just above the naval is the source of your confidence.
- **Root:** Linking you with the earth and the physical world, the root or base chakra controls the energies of your emotional security.
- **Sacral:** In the lower abdomen, the energies relate to emotion, relationships, intuition, and psychic ability.

Draw the chakra points on the illustration opposite and make some notes about their specific energies. You can also see the colors to which each one resonates on the diagram, and deduce the health benefits gained by maintaining a good flow of energy through the chakras.

Crown

_____
_____
_____
_____
_____
_____

Solar plexus

_____
_____
_____
_____
_____
_____

Root

_____
_____
_____
_____
_____
_____

Brow

_____
_____
_____
_____
_____
_____

Sacral

_____
_____
_____
_____
_____
_____

Throat

_____
_____
_____
_____
_____
_____
_____
_____

Heart

_____
_____
_____
_____
_____
_____
_____
_____

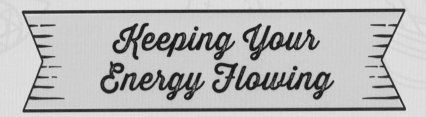

Keeping Your Energy Flowing

The idea behind chakras is that they are the centers through which the energies of your body flow. Any blockages can cause both physical and psychological problems, but you can help to keep them open and the energies flowing freely by using meditation and visualization.

- Define your specific problem and choose a chakra to focus on.
- Cleanse or empower your equipment, if necessary, and cast a circle. Light some candles or incense, if you wish.
- Lie down in a warm and comfortable place within the circle.
- Follow your chosen meditation technique (page 14) to relax completely.
- Watch the energies as though they are a stream flowing around your body. Where do they stop to eddy? Where are they blocked?
- Visualize yourself clearing the stream until it flows smoothly.
- Bring yourself back to full consciousness and try to relate the position of the blockages to your life, so that you know where to focus your attention.

Energy blockages

_____

_____

_____

_____

_____

_____

_____

Energy blockages

_____
_____
_____
_____
_____
_____

Energy blockages

_____
_____
_____
_____
_____
_____
_____

Energy blockages

_____
_____
_____
_____
_____
_____
_____

Water Spells

Spells using water can be cast outdoors on the sea, on a lake or stream, or indoors using a chalice or a bowl of water. Sometimes witches like to add a few drops of essential oil to bring fragrance to bear on the spell.

Correspondences for water spells might be the west, the moon, dusk, autumn, and blue and silver colors. Spells that evoke the powers of water are likely to be concerned with emotional issues, seeking peaceful solutions, and finding the strength to understand and use instinct and internal wisdom. Look at A Spell Template (page 44) and the Table of Correspondences (page 124) and create your own water spells.

Water spell

_____
_____
_____
_____
_____
_____
_____
_____
_____

Water spell

_____
_____
_____
_____

💧 Water spell

💧 Water spell

Mabon—the Energy of Balance

Mabon is the festival of the autumn equinox, when day and night are of equal length but the days are beginning to grow shorter. As the light and dark are in perfect balance, this is a good time for any spellcasting relating to stability and balance.

You may be looking for a better life-work balance, an improvement in the balance of your personal relationship, or a wish to work less hard and ensure that your efforts are valued equally with those of your colleagues. Look at A Spell Template (page 44) and the Table of Correspondences (page 124) and create your own spells to celebrate the autumn equinox.

◇ Mabon spell

_____

_____

_____

_____

_____

_____

_____

_____

_____

◇ Mabon spell

_____

_____

_____

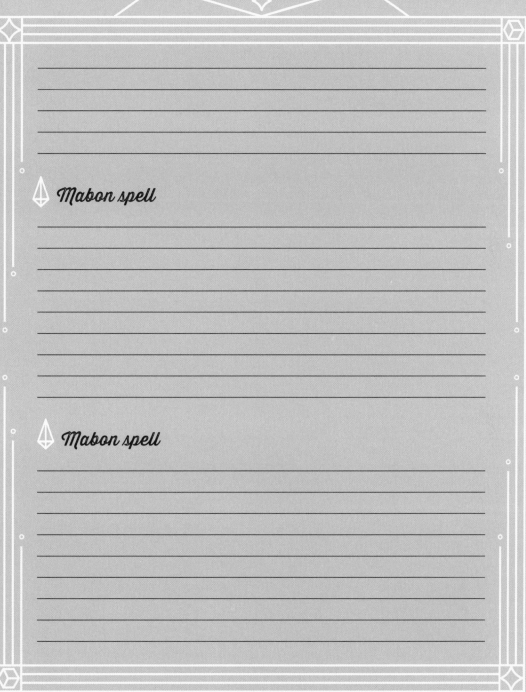

Mabon spell

Mabon spell

To Balance the Elements

Each of us has a different balance of the four elements—earth, air, fire, and water—making up our personality. Our natural sense of balance is unique but if we aim toward the center, then life is likely to be less volatile. Repeating the following ritual every now and again should keep you balanced and centered.

First, choose an item to represent each of the four elements.

Earth

A bowl of salt, sand, or soil, a pentacle, a stone or crystal, or a plant or flower.

Air

A fan, a kite, a bird, wind chimes, or an image of an angel.

Fire

A candle, an image of the sun, an athame, or a statue of a dragon.

Water

A bowl of water, some seashells, or an image of a sea creature.

Next, contemplate each item in turn and let your instincts guide you as to whether you have too much or too little of each particular element.

Too little		Too much
Lacking common sense	**EARTH**	Stubborn
Unhappy	**AIR**	Unable to concentrate
Weak and apathetic	**FIRE**	Prone to anger
Stuck in a rut	**WATER**	Lacking responsibility

If the element is in balance, say:

Element, in balance stay, to see me smoothly on the way.

If you have too little of an element, say:

Element, I call your power, to strengthen in my heart this hour.

If you have too much of an element, say:

Element, abate your strength, to balance my way through at length.

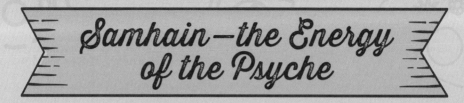

Samhain—the Energy of the Psyche

Among the most important of the sabbats, Samhain falls on the last day of the ancient Celtic calendar, so it is really the start of the witch's year. Samhain is halfway between the equinox and the winter solstice, marking the end of autumn and moving into the darker half of the year.

This is a time to celebrate your achievements and let go of any negative energies that should not be stored to fester over the winter months. Samhain is a good time to cast off the negative, so a windy day is perfect for the leaf spells on page 82.

Look at A Spell Template (page 44) and the Table of Correspondences (page 124) and create your own Samhain spells. You might like to carve a pumpkin or create a spell to bring laughter into your life, or perhaps use fireworks to add strength and excitement.

◇ Samhain spell

_____

_____

_____

_____

_____

_____

_____

◇ Samhain spell

_____

_____

_____
_____
_____
_____
_____
_____

◈ Samhain spell

_____
_____
_____
_____
_____
_____
_____
_____

◈ Samhain spell

_____
_____
_____
_____
_____
_____
_____
_____

Warm Crystals

Crystals can make a significant contribution to your magic, both by their color and texture, as well as their association with the elements, primarily earth. The deeper and darker the color, the stronger the energy relating to the key principle. The examples given below are merely a few of the most popular types of crystal.

Broadly speaking, colors are divided into the warm spectrum (the reds and yellows) and the cool colors (the blues and greens). Warm colors are enlivening and tend to be used for spells of encouragement and strength, such as giving yourself the courage to apply for a new job or to make a major change in your life.

There is also a specific crystal assigned to your birthdate: your birthstone. This can give you additional strength.

Pink

Rose quartz, morganite, kunzite, calcite. Use for spells to cure heartache, develop sensuality, or find romance.

_____

_____

_____

_____

Red

Garnet, carnelian, jasper, bloodstone. Use for spells to build and strengthen, whether for courage, energy, passion, love, or self-esteem.

_____

_____

_____

_____

_____

_____

Orange

Amber, jasper, tiger's eye, sardonyx. Use for spells to promote success using enthusiasm and adventure.

_____

_____

_____

_____

_____

Gold

Pyrites, gold, topaz. Use for spells for happiness and belonging.

_____

_____

_____

_____

Yellow

Citrine, honey calcite, fluorite. Use for spells for clarity and enlightenment.

_____

_____

_____

_____

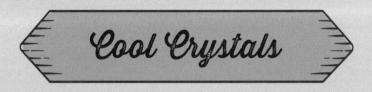

Cool Crystals

The reds and yellows are known as warm colors and are used for empowering and expansive magic. The cool colors (the blues and greens) tend to be more soothing and can be used for magic that instills calm, resolves difficult situations, or clears the way for gentle progress.

When you choose a crystal for a specific purpose, first look carefully at the selection, perhaps narrow it down to the range of colors you are looking for, then let your hand wander over the stones as you think about the spell you are going to use the crystal for. Allow one of the stones to pull you toward it.

Keep your crystal collection somewhere safe and wash the stones regularly, preferably in rainwater, so that they remain at their best.

 ## Green

Aventurine, jade, amazonite, malachite. Use for spells for growth and renewal.

_____

_____

_____

_____

_____

Blue

Aquamarine, blue chalcedony, fluorite, lapis lazuli. Use for spells to promote balance and empathy.

_____

_____

_____

Indigo

Iolite, azurite. Use for spells to engender trust and patience.

_____

_____

_____

Purple

Amethyst, kunzite, lepidolite, sugilite. Use for spells to gain wisdom and maturity.

_____

_____

_____

_____

White

Quartz, moonstone, diamond, selenite. Use for uplifting and positive spells, since white can amplify light and goodness.

_____

_____

_____

Black

Black tourmaline, obsidian, onyx, smoky quartz. Use for grounding and protective spells.

_____

_____

_____

_____

Spells to Break Negative Habits

Spells in this category should be approached with thoughtfulness and care. They can help you to stop negative patterns of behavior or break out of unsuitable peer groups, and they can enhance your self-esteem and confidence in the process, as long as your focus remains on strengthening and defending yourself.

Spells might include wanting to stop smoking or finding the strength to stick to a diet, or simply breaking a habitual pattern. Repetition can be a simple but effective tool here. Write a little mantra to form part of your spell, then keep repeating it to yourself. Here is an example:

> *Active is good, idle is crazy.*
> *If I want to be fit, I cannot be lazy.*

Look at A Spell Template (page 44) and the Table of Correspondences (page 124) and create your own breaking or banishing spells.

Banishing negativity spell

_____

_____

_____

_____

_____

_____

_____

_____

Banishing negativity spell

_____
_____
_____
_____
_____
_____
_____
_____

Banishing negativity spell

_____
_____
_____
_____
_____
_____
_____
_____
_____

A Goddess Talisman

A talisman attracts a particular benefit to the wearer, once it has been charged, consecrated, and dedicated to them. A goddess talisman is designed to increase your confidence in your own abilities.

✧ Choose

When choosing a talisman, a small pendant or piece of jewelry with a representation of the goddess is a popular option. It may come from a particular culture, or you may like to model, carve, or paint your own.

_____

_____

_____

✧ Cleanse

Ideally, your talisman will have no traces of previous energies, so wash it under running water or, if possible, in a fountain or stream. Leave it in a dish of salt overnight, or outdoors under the full moon.

✧ Consecrate

Cast a circle, perhaps light some candles, speak some appropriate words, and ask your talisman to channel the universal energies to your subconscious. Call on the elements and give thanks to the goddess:

Mother Earth, help me be strong
When I need your grounding, please come along.

I call the air, so fresh and clean
To surround me with a protective sheen.

Strength of fire, come to me
To build my courage because of thee.

Water, smooth my path, I ask
For guidance clear, not in a mask.

Goddess kind and true, be there
For me, in everywhere.

_____

_____

_____

_____

_____

_____

_____

_____

_____

_____

_____

> An amulet can be charged in the same way, but is designed to ward off negative influences. You might choose your birthstone or perhaps a gift from a loved one.

Herbs and Spices in Magic

Closely aligned to fragrance but bringing in the elements of growth and development, herbs and spices can be used in a variety of ways, such as healing, calming, and protection. If you have an outdoor altar, you may want to grow some herbs nearby, either from seed or from small plants. When working with herbs, cleanse all your equipment before you begin.

Tisanes—or teas—can be made from many kinds of herbs. To make a delicious Middle Eastern-style drink that refreshes the mind and spirit, pour boiling water onto a large handful of mint, then add sugar to taste. Chamomile tea is relaxing, while peppermint tea is invigorating.

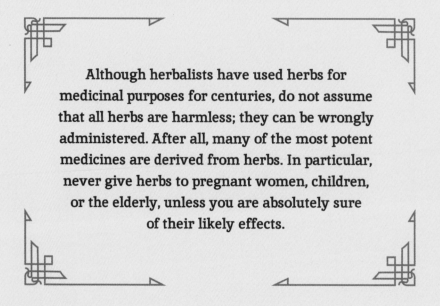

Although herbalists have used herbs for medicinal purposes for centuries, do not assume that all herbs are harmless; they can be wrongly administered. After all, many of the most potent medicines are derived from herbs. In particular, never give herbs to pregnant women, children, or the elderly, unless you are absolutely sure of their likely effects.

Allspice

A spice mixture that promotes prosperity.

Basil

A protective herb also used to promote calm.

Angelica

For protection.

Chamomile

For harmony and healing.

Mint

To stimulate body and mind.

Marigold

For prosperity and contentment.

Ginger

Produces a calming effect.

Dill

To promote good luck.

Cinnamon

An energizing spice used for uplifting in just about any context.

Caraway

For protection and to dispel negativity.

Sage

For magical protection.

Rosemary

For protection and healing.

Spells for Children and Family

Anyone who is a parent will know that they never stop wanting to protect their children, whether their offspring are aged five or fifty! When making spells for children, look for images of youth and beauty, safe places and protection, but also self-esteem and confidence.

Spells might include helping a child cope with bullying, supporting them in making a decision about a course, giving them the confidence to speak out against peer pressure, or simply helping them to be themselves. Spells for the family might relate to many of the other spells in this book, so first decide on the single most important factor in your spell. Do you want to bless and maintain an existing strong unit, resolve differences, or find a way to reunite after a family problem?

Look at A Spell Template (page 44) and the Table of Correspondences (page 124) and create spells for those closest to you. Always stay positive, and take strength from your magic if you need to deal with a problem yourself to resolve an issue. Actions to include in family spells might involve using tarot cards, candles, or herbs.

Spell for a child

_____

_____

_____

_____

_____

_____

_____

_____

Spell for the family

_____
_____
_____
_____
_____
_____
_____

Spell for a child

_____
_____
_____
_____
_____
_____
_____
_____
_____

Spell for the family

_____
_____
_____
_____
_____
_____
_____
_____
_____

Knot Magic

If you feel that something is holding you back or you have a problem to which you cannot find a solution, it may be helpful to bring some knot magic into your spells.

Choose a cord in a color suitable for the spell you are going to cast. It doesn't need to be very long—just enough to tie a series of knots along its length. Cleanse or empower the cord with your other magical items, then open the circle and awaken the elements. Tie as many knots along the length of the cord as there are aspects of your problem. As you tie each one, state each part of the problem clearly and concisely. Take a knife or scissors and cut through each of the knots, stating a solution or asking that the issue be resolved. Bury the pieces of cord while saying:

Below the ground rest, out of harm's way.
You'll not be needed for many a day.
An it harm none, do as you will.

✦ Knot spell

_____
_____
_____
_____
_____
_____
_____
_____

✦ Knot spell

_____
_____
_____
_____
_____
_____
_____
_____

✦ Knot spell

_____
_____
_____
_____
_____
_____
_____
_____

✦ Knot spell

_____
_____
_____
_____
_____
_____
_____
_____
_____

Yule—the Energy of Celebration

For thousands of years, witches have celebrated the winter solstice with the sabbat of Yule, when the day is shortest and the night is longest. In the northern hemisphere, this was absorbed into Christmas celebrations, and this highlights the confluence of pagan, Christian, and other traditions around the world.

You might think about exploring more deeply how pagan and other traditions have evolved and combined.

An altar is an important part of Yule tradition. Start by decorating your altar in a red cloth with green sprigs of holly or mistletoe and some red candles. Spells are favored that deal with positivity and celebrating all the good things that bring joy into your life.

Pagan traditions

_____

_____

_____

_____

_____

_____

_____

_____

_____

Other traditions

_____

_____

_____

_____

_____

_____

_____

_____

_____

Earth Spells

There are so many correspondences which can be used to symbolize the element of earth that it is always easy to find something appropriate to use when making an earth spells. It is a good idea to ring the changes and use different substances or items in your spells, otherwise you will never find out whether one is more effective for you than another.

Salt, soil, or sand can all be used. Any plant, flower, or vegetable also makes a good earth symbol, as do crystals and gemstones.

⊕ Earth spell

_____

_____

_____

_____

_____

_____

_____

_____

_____

⊕ Earth spell

_____

_____

_____

_____

_____

_____

_____

_____

_____

⊕ *Earth spell*

_____

_____

_____

_____

_____

_____

_____

_____

_____

_____

⊕ *Earth spell*

_____

_____

_____

_____

_____

_____

_____

_____

_____

_____

_____

The Road Goes Ever Onward

Witchcraft has grown organically around the world and in many different cultures, absorbing activities from one era to the next. As you further your studies, you may discover links between celebrations on different continents or among peoples who seemingly have no connection. A web search on the internet can throw up all sorts of interesting links that warrant further investigation.

_____   _____   _____

_____   _____   _____

_____   _____   _____

_____   _____   _____

                        _____

_____   _____   _____

_____   _____   _____

                                                _____

For example, people in the UK and USA celebrate Halloween, while in Mexico they celebrate _Día de Muertos_ or the "Day of the Dead." In European traditions, witches often kept cats as familiars to help them with their magic. In Native American cultures, warriors—or braves— were said to be imbued with the strength of their animal spirit guides.

There is no end to the study of witchcraft and learning to be at one with the natural world. Whether you are new to the craft or have been practicing for some time, hopefully you have found it has affected your life in a positive way. A good way to assess how you are progressing is to do an informal review of your activities and achievements. You don't need to have scaled Mount Everest; just be thankful for the small things that are most significant to you.

★ *Events*

_____

★ *Friendships*

_____

★ *Self-esteem*

_____

★ *Understanding of self and others*

_____

★ *Ability to communicate effectively*

_____

★ *Low points and how you dealt with them*

_____

★ *High points and their impact*

_____

★ *Resolutions moving forward*

_____

Table of Correspondences

When you are spellcasting, you are looking to include items in your spells that resonate with energies, each helping to achieve your goal. Ultimately your choices will be personal, but these tables, based around the sabbats and the elements, provide some starting points.

Sabbat	Festival	Relevant spell themes	Position of the sun	Symbols
Yule	Midwinter celebration of rebirth	Growth, nurturing, strength, peace, love, hope	Winter solstice	Holly, evergreens, mistletoe
Imbolc	Beginning of spring	Awakening, cleansing, protection, the young, creativity	Between winter solstice and spring equinox	St Brigid, sheep, swan, serpent
Ostara	Height of spring	Growth and development, expanding horizons, balance	Spring equinox	Flowers (especially bulbs), eggs, rabbits
Beltaine	Beginning of summer	Growth, fertility, love, prosperity	Between spring equinox and summer solstice	Chalices, the goddess and the god, growing things

Colors	Crystals	Flowers and fragrances	Season	Direction
Green, red	Bloodstone, emerald, garnet, ruby	Rosemary, cinnamon, frankincense, myrrh, pine	Winter	North
White, red, black	Amethyst, sunstone, ruby, onyx	Lavender, chamomile, rosemary	Winter–spring	North-east
Yellow, green	Moonstone, jasper, citrine, chrysoprase	Honeysuckle, jasmine, rose	Spring	East
Green, red, silver	Citrine, tiger's eye, emerald, amber	Rose, lilac, frankincense, vanilla	Spring–summer	South-east

Sabbat	Festival	Relevant spell themes	Position of the sun	Symbols
Litha	Height of summer	Passion, courage, learning, awareness	Summer solstice	Flowers, candles, cauldron, sun symbols
Lammas	First harvest	Prosperity, harvest, transformation, change	Between summer solstice and autumn equinox	Grapes, wine, garlands, corn dollies
Mabon	Fruitfulness of the harvest	Self-confidence, prosperity, security, intuition, emotion, friendship, hospitality	Autumn equinox	Cornucopia, wheels
Samhain	Beginning of winter and the dark of the year	Divination, feasting, sensuality	Between autumn equinox and winter solstice	Pumpkins, black cats, bonfires